Life in the Time of

# Abraham Lincoln
# and the
# Civil War

## Revised Edition

capstone

To contact Capstone Global Library, please
call 800-747-4992, or visit our website
www.mycapstone.com

Designed by Kimberly R. Miracle and Betsy Wernert.

**Library of Congress Cataloging-in-Publication Data**
is available on the Library of Congress website.
978-1-4846-3822-4 (revised paperback)
978-1-4846-3890-3 (ebook pdf)

**Acknowledgments**
Alamy: Historic Florida, 10, Niday Picture Library, 16; Capstone Press, 6-7; Getty Images: Afro Newspaper/Gado, 19, Bettmann, 20, 24, Hulton Archive, 26; iStockphoto: HultonArchive, 17; Library of Congress: Prints and Photographs Division Washington, top left cover, bottom cover, 12; National Archives and Records Administration, 8; Newscom: Images Distribution/Agence Quebec Presse, 14; Shutterstock: Everett Historical, 4, 5, 9, 11, 18, 21, 22, 23, 25, 27, Mark Carrel, 15; SuperStock, 13

Map illustrations on pages 6 and 7 by Mapping Specialists, Ltd.

Every effort has been made to contact copyright holders of any material reproduced in this book. Any omissions will be rectified in subsequent printings if notice is given to the publisher.

**Disclaimer**
All Internet addresses (URLs) given in this book were valid at the time of going to press. However, due to the dynamic nature of the Internet, some addresses may have changed or ceased to exist since publication. While the author and the publishers regret any inconvenience this may cause readers, no responsibility for any such changes can be accepted by either the author or the publishers.

# Contents

Some words are shown in bold, **like this**. You can find out what they mean by looking in the glossary.

# Meet Abraham Lincoln

Abraham Lincoln was the 16th president of the United States. He was born in Kentucky on February 12, 1809. His family lived in a log cabin on the **frontier**. They did not have a lot of money.

Abraham Lincoln grew up in this log cabin.

Abraham Lincoln was president from 1861 to 1865.

As a boy, Abraham Lincoln only had about one year of school. As a teenager, he worked many different jobs. He moved to Illinois with his family when he was 21 years old. In 1834, when he was 25 years old, he was **elected** to the Illinois state government.

# A Young Country

The United States at this time was a young country. Less than 100 years before, it had been ruled by Great Britain. The United States had fought against British rule. It had won its **independence** and become its own country.

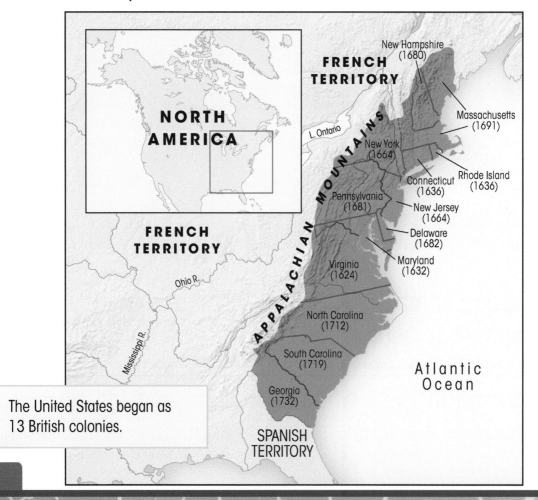

NORTH AMERICA

FRENCH TERRITORY

FRENCH TERRITORY

L. Ontario

Ohio R.

Mississippi R.

APPALACHIAN MOUNTAINS

New Hampshire (1680)

Massachusetts (1691)

New York (1664)

Rhode Island (1636)

Connecticut (1636)

Pennsylvania (1681)

New Jersey (1664)

Delaware (1682)

Maryland (1632)

Virginia (1624)

North Carolina (1712)

South Carolina (1719)

Georgia (1732)

Atlantic Ocean

SPANISH TERRITORY

The United States began as 13 British colonies.

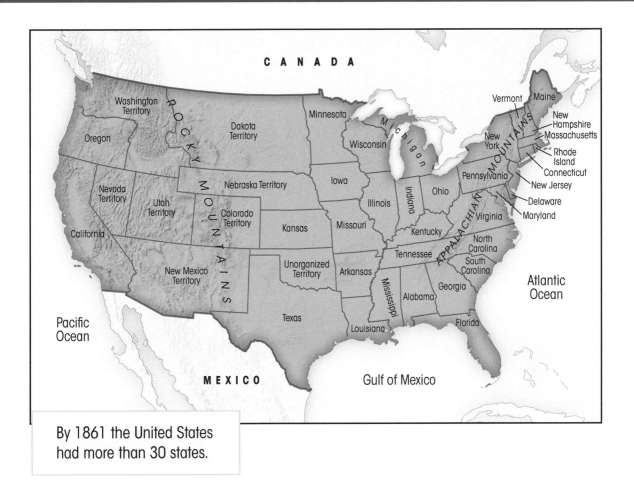

By 1861 the United States had more than 30 states.

At first, the United States had only 13 states. Soon other parts of **North America** became states. Kentucky, where Abraham Lincoln was born, became a state in 1792. Illinois became a state in 1818.

# Slavery in the United States

Some laws in the United States had to be followed by all the states. These laws were written down in the United States **Constitution**. The early leaders did not want one big government to have too much power. So states could also make their own laws.

The U.S. Constitution was written in 1787.

Slaves were bought and sold.

The early leaders could not agree about **slavery**. Slavery is when one person owns another person. The slave is forced to work very hard and do what the owner says. The early leaders decided to let each state make its own laws about slavery.

# On the Plantation

Plantation owners lived in big houses and had a lot of money.

Most states in the North made **slavery illegal**, but most states in the South made slavery **legal**. Southern states had large **plantations**. Plantation owners grew cotton, tobacco, and other **crops**. They needed slaves to work in the plantation fields.

Working on the plantation was very hard. Slaves worked all day in the hot fields, picking crops like cotton. Slaves could not leave the plantation. They had to work all the time.

Slaves were not paid for the work they did.

# A Country Divided

Many slaves escaped their hard life. They traveled to states in the North where **slavery** was **illegal**. Many people helped the escaped slaves. Many people thought slavery should be illegal everywhere.

Harriet Tubman was a slave from Maryland who escaped in 1849.

Plantation owners were afraid they would lose money if slaves did not work in the fields.

Many people in the South did not agree. They needed the slaves to work on the **plantations**. They did not think the United States government should tell the states what to do. They thought each state should decide what was best for it.

# The Confederate States of America

The Southern states decided that they should form their own country. They broke away from the United States, or the **Union**. In December of 1860, South Carolina was the first state to break away.

Jefferson Davis was chosen president of the Confederate States.

Six more states followed: Alabama, Florida, Georgia, Louisiana, Mississippi, and Texas. Together they formed a new country called the Confederate States of America. Virginia, North Carolina, Tennessee, and Arkansas would also **join** the **Confederacy**.

The Confederate States of America created its own money.

# The Civil War

In 1861 soldiers for the **Confederate** Army **attacked** Fort Sumter in South Carolina. They fought against **Union** soldiers. The Civil War had begun. The Union Army of the United States was fighting the Confederate Army of the Confederate States.

The first battle of the Civil War was at Fort Sumter.

Union soldiers wore dark blue uniforms.
Confederate soldiers wore gray uniforms.

Abraham Lincoln became president in 1861. He thought **slavery** was wrong. He also wanted the country to stay together. Americans were fighting against Americans, and thousands of people were dying.

# Proclaiming Freedom

Abraham Lincoln had not wanted a war. He still believed that the slaves should be free. In the fall of 1862, he wrote the Emancipation Proclamation.

The Emancipation Proclamation became official on January 1, 1863.

The slaves no longer had to work in the **plantation** fields.

To emancipate something means to free it. To proclaim something means to tell everyone. The Emancipation Proclamation told everyone that the slaves in the **Confederate** states were free.

# A Battle at Gettysburg

About 50,000 soldiers were hurt, captured, or killed in the Battle of Gettysburg.

From July 1 to July 3 of 1863, a large battle took place in Gettysburg, Pennsylvania. Thousands of **Union** and **Confederate** soldiers fought each other. In the end, the Union Army won. It was an important **victory**.

The place where the battle happened became a **cemetery**. It honored all the soldiers who had died there. On November 19, 1863, President Lincoln gave an important speech there. His speech is called the Gettysburg Address.

The Gettysburg Address honored the soldiers who had died.

# Fighting for Freedom

For black Americans, the Civil War was a fight for **freedom**. If the **Union** won, **slavery** would end. Thousands of black soldiers signed up to fight. Some were escaped slaves, and others were free blacks from the North.

After the Emancipation Proclamation, many black Americans decided to fight in the Civil War.

About 180,000 black Americans fought for the Union during the Civil War. The black soldiers fought well and hard. They earned the respect of the white soldiers.

Sixteen black soldiers won the highest military award in the United States—the Congressional Medal of Honor.

# The Confederacy Surrenders

After the Battle of Gettysburg, many more battles were fought. The war continued for almost two more years. The **Union** Army kept winning. It was beating the **Confederate** Army.

Many Southern cities were destroyed during the Civil War.

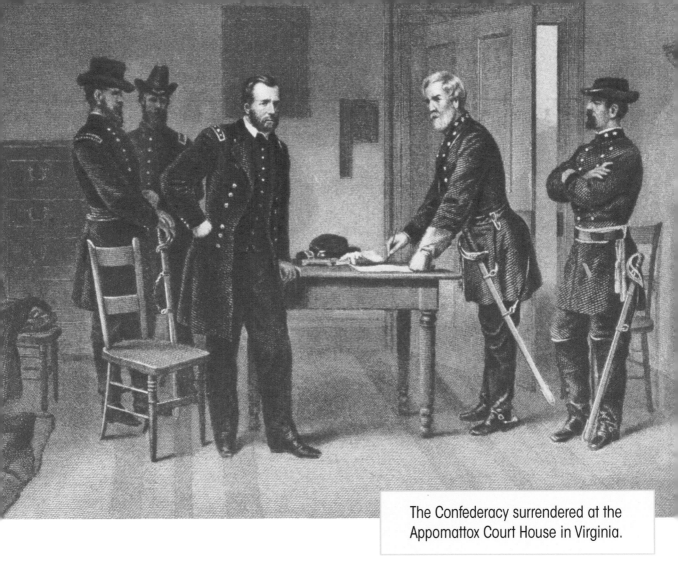

The Confederacy surrendered at the Appomattox Court House in Virginia.

In 1864 Abraham Lincoln was **elected** president again. On April 9, 1865, the Confederate Army **surrendered** to the Union Army. The Civil War was over. The United States was one country again.

# No More Slavery

The Civil War kept the United States together. It helped to free the slaves. A change was made to the United States **Constitution** on December 6, 1865. The change said that **slavery** was **illegal** in every state.

The 13th Amendment to the U.S. Constitution made slavery illegal.

President Lincoln was killed a few days after the Civil War ended.

The Civil War was an important war, but many people died. Around 600,000 soldiers died. Abraham Lincoln died, too. A man named John Wilkes Booth shot President Lincoln on April 14, 1865.

# If You Grew Up Long Ago

If you grew up in the time of Abraham Lincoln…

- You could not call your family and friends because there were no telephones.

- You would learn about war battles days after they happened because there were no radios or televisions.

- You would need to ride horses to get quickly from place to place because there were no cars.

- You would have to light your home with candles.

- You could not record important speeches, so you would have to write them down by hand.

# Timeline

**1809**   Abraham Lincoln is born.

**1834**   Abraham Lincoln is **elected** to the Illinois state government.

**1860**   Southern states begin to break away from the United States, or the **Union**.

**1861**   Abraham Lincoln becomes president of the United States.

April: The first battle of the Civil War is fought at Fort Sumter in South Carolina.

**1862**   President Lincoln writes the Emancipation Proclamation.

**1863**   July: The Battle of Gettysburg is fought in Pennsylvania.

November: President Lincoln gives his speech, the Gettysburg Address, at the Gettysburg battlefield.

**1865**   Abraham Lincoln becomes president of the United States a second time.

April 9: The **Confederacy surrenders**. The Civil War is over.

April 14: President Lincoln is shot. He dies the next morning.

December: The 13th Amendment makes **slavery illegal**.

# Find Out More

## Books

Binns, Tristan Boyer. *The Lincoln Memorial*. Heinemann Library, 2001.

Burke, Rick. *Abraham Lincoln*. Chicago: Heinemann Library, 2003.

Feinstein, Stephen. *Read About Abraham Lincoln*. Berkeley Heights, NJ: Enslow, 2004.

Mara, Wil. *Harriet Tubman*. New York: Children's Press, 2002.

## Internet Sites

FactHound offers a safe, fun way to find Internet sites related to this book. All of the sites on FactHound have been researched by our staff.

Visit *www.facthound.com*

# Glossary

**attack** try to hurt someone by fighting

**cemetery** place where people who have died are buried

**Confederacy** group of Southern states that fought against the United States in the Civil War

**Confederate** having to do with the Confederacy

**constitution** written document that tell the rights of people and the powers of the government in a country

**crop** plant grown by farmers for food and other uses

**elect** choose someone by voting

**freedom** right to do and say what you want

**frontier** far edge of a place, where not many people live

**join** come together

**illegal** against the law

**independence** not belonging to another country or group of people

**legal** allowed by the law; okay to do something

**North America** one of the seven continents, or large pieces of land, on Earth

**plantation** large farm, usually where it is warm, where crops like cotton and tobacco are grown

**slavery** when someone is owned and forced to work for another person

**surrender** give up in a war or battle

**Union** another word for the United States of America

**victory** win in a battle or contest

# Index